Crabbing With Granddad
By Amy MacWilliams Schisler

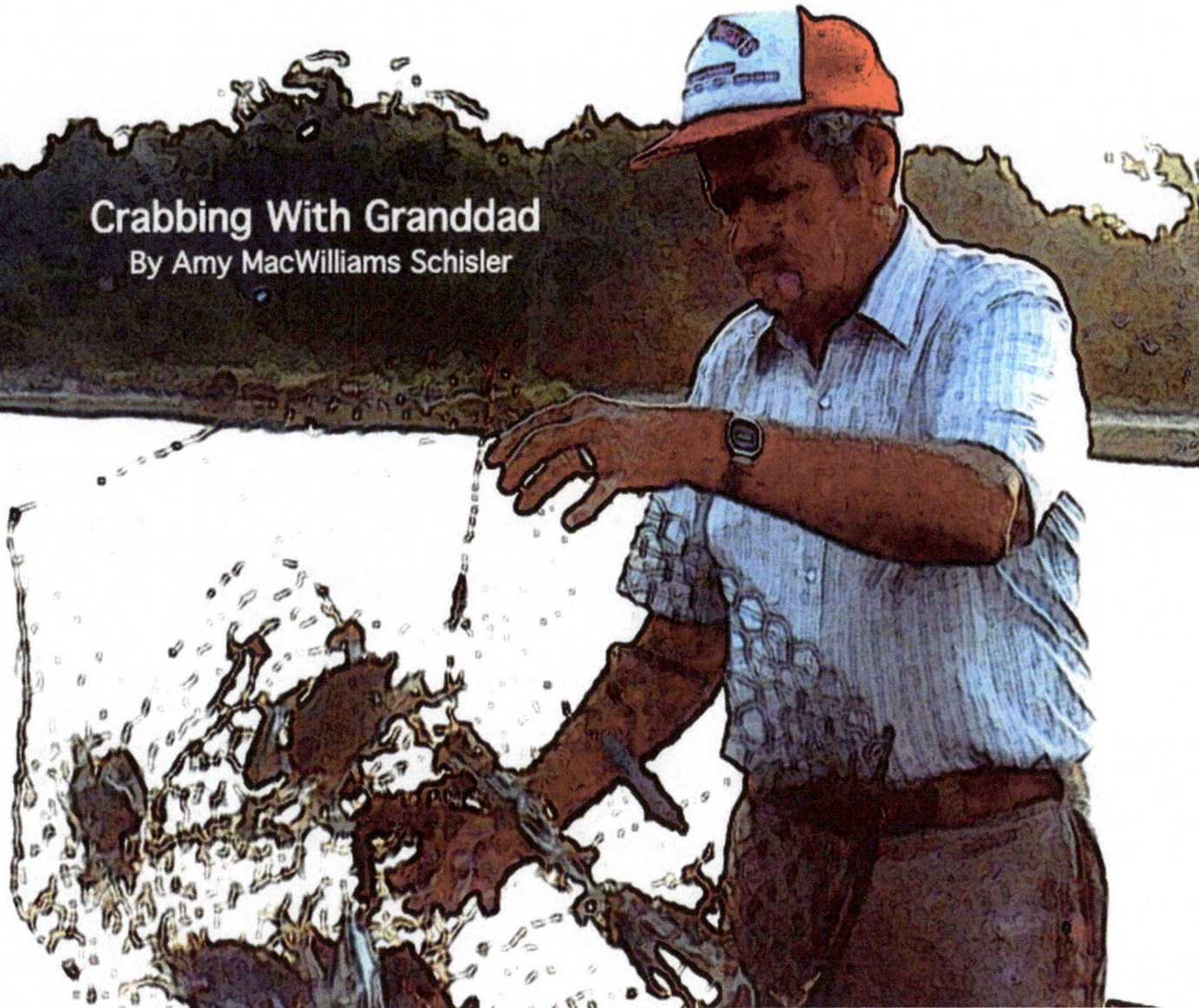

ISBN-13: 979-8-9852232-5-5

Published by:
Chesapeake Sunrise Publishing
Amy Schisler
Bozman, MD
2022

Dedicated to my grandfather, Eugene (Buck) Morgan
who was my hero.

Crabbing With Granddad
By
Amy Schisler

2022
Bozman, MD

When I was a little girl, I spent a lot of time at my grandparents' house in the country. My favorite thing to do was to go crabbing with Granddad.

One morning, Grandma woke my brothers and me just as the sun came up. We dressed and ate quickly and then helped Granddad load the bushel baskets into his big yellow truck.

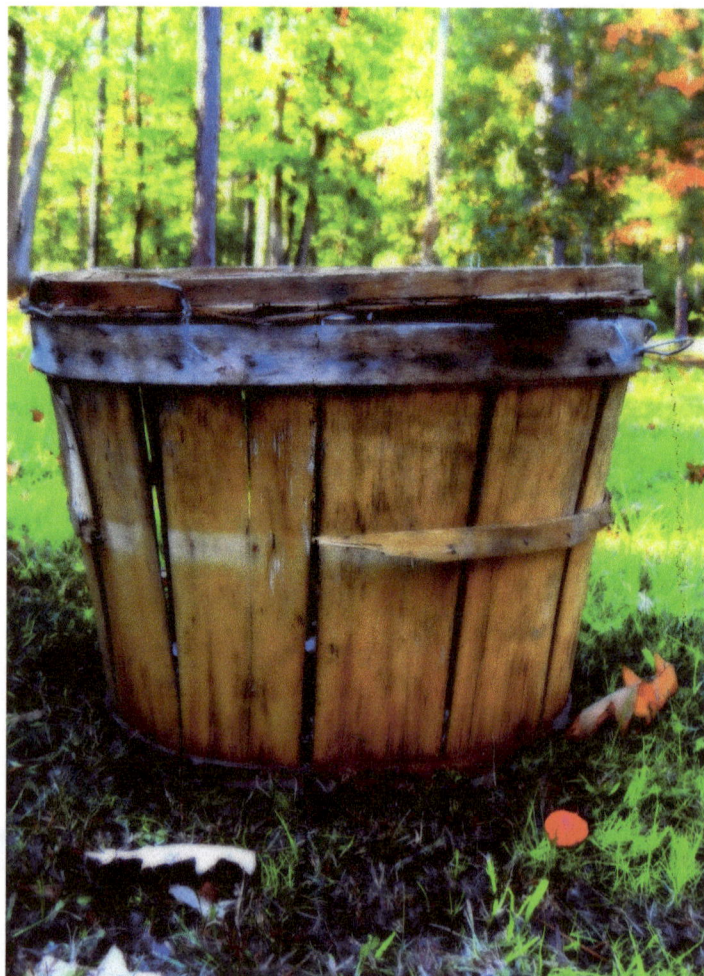

Then we drove past fields of *tobacco* on our way down to the river. Farmers waved to us as we passed by the sweet-smelling fields.

We went to the *pier* where Granddad kept his *skiff*. I put on my lifejacket while Granddad put our snacks into the little boat he had built with his own hands.

Granddad was tall and tanned with a lot of hair, and I thought he was the bravest man in the world.

Granddad spotted his first *crab pot* and pulled it up. It was like a treasure box being pulled from the ocean, filled with beautiful blue crabs.
"I see one!" I yelled as I spied the next pot.

Granddad let me pull up a pot full of crabs.
"I want to pull up one," said my brother, Scott.
"You're next," said Granddad.

"Look!" I shouted as I lifted my third pot from the water. It had a *doubler* in it. That's a male crab, called a *jimmy*, that is protecting a female *soft crab* from harm until she changes to a *paper shell* and then her shell hardens. Granddad threw the female crab back into the water. Later, the female will lay eggs.

Granddad put all of the crabs into the *culling box* except for the soft crabs and *peelers*. He kept those separate so Grandma could cook soft crabs for my dad when he came to pick us up. The peelers would go into the *float* back at the dock.

As Granddad separated the crabs, he asked us questions to see if we remembered what he had taught us about the crab's life cycle.

"Is this a boy or girl?" he asked about the one with the bright red claws and an apron on her belly that was shaped like the U.S. Capitol building. We knew that she was called a *sook*.

After our snack, we took turns steering the boat. I went first, then Scott, then Michael. While we drove, Granddad culled the crabs, keeping the big crabs and throwing the small ones back into the water.

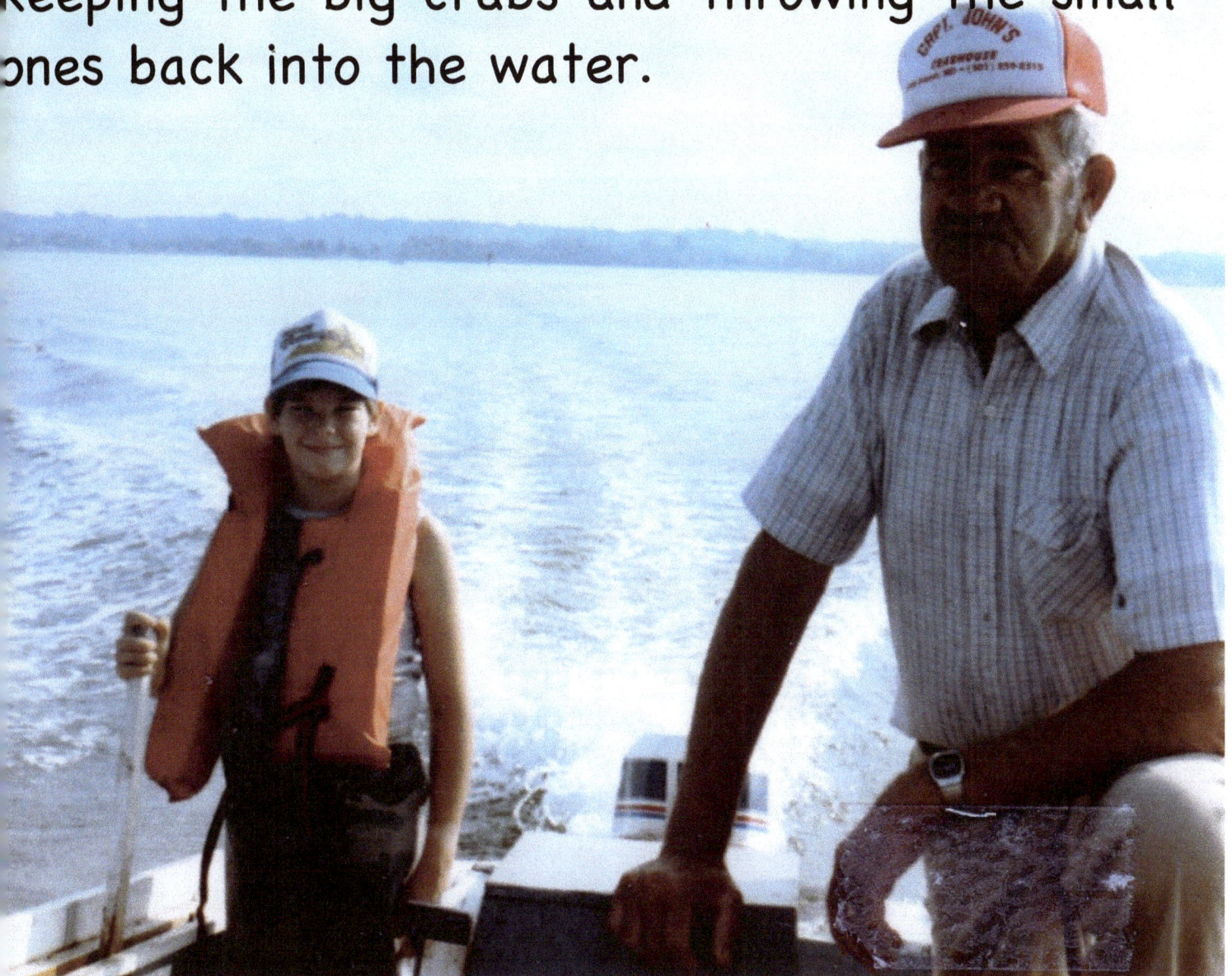

We sold most of our catch but kept enough to eat. When we got to the dock, we unloaded the boat before climbing into the truck and heading home. We couldn't wait to show Grandma our crabs.

Back at the house, Grandma looked at the crabs in our basket.

"Nice catch, kids," she said. "Those are some beautiful crabs."

Granddad filled the big steaming pot with the crabs so that they could cook, and we went inside to eat lunch.

That night, we ate the crabs and talked about our wonderful adventure on the water.

Early the next morning, as the sun came up, Granddad's yellow truck headed down the road with three children in the back seat.

We couldn't wait for another morning...

Crabbing With Granddad.

Glossary

Culling Box - a box used to hold live blue crabs after they are pulled from the water but before they are measured.

Crab pot - a metal cube-shaped box made out of chicken wire that is used to catch hard crabs.

Doubler - a male crab carrying a female peeler in his claws as part of the mating process.

Float - a floating wooden box used to hold live crabs, usually peelers, in the water. After the peelers become soft crabs, they can be cooked and eaten.

Jimmy - a male crab.

Paper Shell - a soft crab whose shell is in the process of hardening.

Peeler - a crab that is getting ready to shed its hard shell and become a soft crab.

Soft Crab - a crab that has shed its hard shell and has yet to harden again.

Skiff - a small wooden boat used by watermen.

Sook - a female crab.

Tobacco – a crop that was once the cash crop of Maryland but is not grown on many farms any longer.

Wharf - A wooden structure extending from the shore out above the water (also known as a pier). Boats or skiffs are tied to it.